SUPPORT
HEART HEALTH
and Maintain Wellness
for a Healthy
Lifestyle.

Lower Cholesterol

Naturally

FULL
COLOR

Phyllis L Padgett

BREAKFAST

LUNCH

DINNER

SNACK

SMOKY COD, BROCCOLI & ORZO BAKE

Prep Time: 10 mins
Cook time: 20 mins
Servings: 2

NUTRITION

Kcal: 618
Fat: 6g
Saturates: 1g
Carbs: 78g
Sugars: 18g
Fibre: 11g
Protein: 57g
Salt: 1.3g

INGREDIENTS

- ½ tbsp olive oil, plus a drizzle
- 1 onion, chopped
- 1 tsp smoked paprika, plus a pinch
- ½-1 tbsp chipotle paste
- 200g long-stem broccoli
- 400ml hot vegetable stock
- 150g orzo
- ½ small bunch of dill, chopped
- ½ small bunch of parsley, chopped
- 50g frozen peas
- 2 sustainable skinless cod fillets
- 4 tbsp fat-free yogurt

DIRECTION

1. Step 1: Preheat the oven to 200°C (180°C fan, gas mark 6). In a deep ovenproof frying pan, heat oil and fry the onion for 5 minutes until tender. Add paprika, chipotle paste, broccoli, and stock, then stir in the orzo. Transfer the pan to the oven and bake for 10 minutes.
2. Step 2: Stir in half of the herbs and the peas. Nestle the fish into the orzo mixture, sprinkle a pinch of paprika on top, drizzle with oil, and season. Bake for another 8-10 minutes until the fish is cooked through and the orzo is tender. In a separate bowl, mix the remaining herbs with yogurt, loosening with a little water if needed. Serve the herb-yogurt mixture with the baked orzo and fish.

JAMIE'S SWEET AND EASY CORN ON THE COB

Prep Time: 20 mins

Cook time: 5 mins

Servings: 8

INGREDIENTS

- 2 tablespoons white sugar
- 1 tablespoon lemon juice
- 6 ears corn on the cob, husks and silk removed

NUTRITION

Calories: 94
Fat: 1g
Carbs: 22g
Protein: 3g

DIRECTION

1. Fill a large pot about 3/4 full of water and bring to a boil. Stir in sugar and lemon juice until sugar is dissolved.
2. Gently place ears of corn into boiling water, cover the pot, turn off the heat, and let corn cook in the hot water until tender, about 10 minutes.

SARAH'S HOMEMADE APPLESAUCE

Prep Time: 10 mins

Cook time: 15 mins

Servings: 4

INGREDIENTS

- 4 apples - peeled, cored and chopped
- ¾ cup water
- ¼ cup white sugar
- ½ teaspoon ground cinnamon

NUTRITION

Calories: 121
Fat: 0g
Carbs: 32g
Protein: 0g

DIRECTION

1. Combine apples, water, sugar, and cinnamon in a saucepan; cover and cook over medium heat until apples are soft, about 15 to 20 minutes.
2. Allow apple mixture to cool, then mash with a fork or potato masher until it is the consistency you like.

BEST SPANISH RICE

Prep Time: 10 mins

Cook time: 20 mins

Servings: 5

INGREDIENTS

- 2 tablespoons oil
- 2 tablespoons chopped onion
- 1 ½ cups uncooked white rice
- 2 cups chicken broth
- 1 cup picante sauce

NUTRITION

Calories: 286
Fat: 6g
Carbs: 51g
Protein: 6g

DIRECTION

1. Heat oil in a large, heavy skillet over medium heat. Add onion; cook and stir until tender, about 5 minutes.
2. Add rice; cook and stir until rice begins to turn golden brown. Stir in chicken broth and picante sauce. Reduce heat, cover, and simmer until liquid has been absorbed, about 15 to 20 minutes.

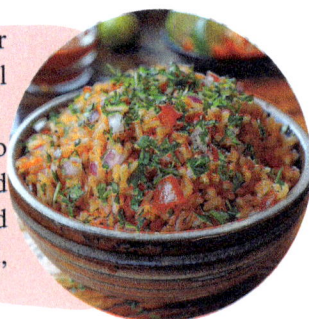

APPLE CINNAMON OATMEAL

Prep Time: 5 mins

Cook time: 5 mins

Servings: 2

INGREDIENTS

- 1 cup water
- ¼ cup apple juice
- 1 apple, cored and chopped
- ⅔ cup rolled oats
- 1 teaspoon ground cinnamon
- 1 cup milk

NUTRITION

Calories: 217
Fat: 4g
Carbs: 38g
Protein: 8g

DIRECTION

1. Combine water, apple juice, and apples in a saucepan. Bring to a boil over high heat; stir in rolled oats and cinnamon. Return to a boil, then reduce heat to low, and simmer until thick, about 3 minutes. Spoon into serving bowls, and add milk.

PEACHY OATMEAL

Prep Time: 5 mins

Cook time: 3 mins

Servings: 1

INGREDIENTS

- ½ (15 ounce) can sliced peaches, drained
- ½ cup water
- ½ cup milk
- ½ cup quick-cooking oats
- 2 tablespoons packed brown sugar
- ¼ teaspoon ground cinnamon, or more to taste
- 1 pinch salt

NUTRITION

Calories: 411
Fat: 5g
Carbs: 85g
Protein: 11g

DIRECTION

1. Stir peaches, water, milk, oats, brown sugar, cinnamon, and salt together in a microwave-safe bowl.
2. Cook in microwave on High, stirring every 60 seconds, until the oats are softened, about 3 minutes. Stir one final time before serving.

BUTTERSCOTCH OATMEAL

Prep Time: 5 mins

Cook time: 10 mins

Servings: 3

INGREDIENTS

- 1 egg, beaten
- 1 ¾ cups milk
- ½ cup packed brown sugar
- 1 cup rolled oats
- 2 tablespoons butter

NUTRITION

Calories: 357
Fat: 14g
Carbs: 49g
Protein: 11g

DIRECTION

1. In a saucepan over medium heat, whisk together the egg, milk and brown sugar. Mix in the oats. When the oatmeal begins to boil, cook and stir until thick. Remove from the heat, and stir in butter until melted. Serve immediately.

HEALTHY COCONUT OATMEAL

🕐 Prep Time: 5 mins

🕐 Cook time: 10 mins

🍴 Servings: 6

INGREDIENTS

- 3 ½ cups plain or vanilla soy milk
- ¼ teaspoon salt
- 2 cups rolled oats
- ¼ cup pure maple syrup
- ⅓ cup raisins
- ⅓ cup dried cranberries
- ⅓ cup sweetened flaked coconut
- ⅓ cup chopped walnuts
- 1 (8 ounce) container plain yogurt (Optional)
- 3 tablespoons honey (Optional)

NUTRITION

Calories: 379
Fat: 10g
Carbs: 63g
Protein: 12g

DIRECTION

1. Pour the milk and salt into a saucepan, and bring to a boil. Stir in the oats, maple syrup, raisins, and cranberries. Return to a boil, then reduce heat to medium. Cook for 5 minutes. Stir in walnuts and coconut, and let stand until it reaches your desired thickness. Spoon into serving bowls, and top with yogurt and honey, if desired.

SPINACH, SWEET POTATO & LENTIL DHAL

Prep Time: 10 mins
Cook time: 35 mins

Servings: 4

NUTRITION

Kcal: 397
Fat: 5g
Saturates: 1g
Carbs: 65g
Sugars: 19g
Fibre: 11g
Protein: 18g
Salt: 0.6g

INGREDIENTS

- 1 tbsp sesame oil
- 1 red onion, finely chopped
- 1 garlic clove, crushed
- thumb-sized piece ginger, peeled and finely chopped
- 1 red chilli, finely chopped
- 1½ tsp ground turmeric
- 1½ tsp ground cumin
- 2 sweet potatoes (about 400g/14oz), cut into even chunks
- 250g red split lentils
- 600ml vegetable stock
- 80g bag of spinach
- 4 spring onions, sliced on the diagonal, to serve
½ small pack of Thai basil, leaves torn, to serve

11

DIRECTION

1. Heat 1 tablespoon of sesame oil in a pan with a tight lid.
2. Sauté 1 finely chopped red onion on low heat for 10 minutes until it softens.
3. Add 1 crushed garlic clove, finely chopped ginger, and 1 red chili. Cook for 1 minute, then add 1½ teaspoons each of turmeric and cumin, and cook for another minute.
4. Increase heat to medium, add 2 chunked sweet potatoes, and mix well with the spices.
5. Add 250g red split lentils and 600ml vegetable stock. Season as desired.
6. Bring to a boil, then simmer covered for 20 minutes until the lentils are tender and the potatoes maintain their shape.
7. Adjust seasoning, then stir in 80g spinach until wilted. Garnish with sliced spring onions and torn basil leaves.
8. Optionally, let the dish cool, then store in airtight containers in the fridge for a healthy meal option later.

HEATHER'S GRILLED SALMON

Prep Time: 10 mins
Cook time: 10 mins
Servings: 4

NUTRITION

Calories: 379
Fat: 10g
Carbs: 63g
Protein: 12g

INGREDIENTS

- ¼ cup brown sugar
- ¼ cup olive oil
- ¼ cup soy sauce
- 2 teaspoons lemon pepper
- 1 teaspoon dried thyme
- 1 teaspoon dried basil
- 1 teaspoon dried parsley
- ½ teaspoon garlic powder
- 4 (6 ounce) salmon fillets

DIRECTION

1. Whisk together the brown sugar, olive oil, soy sauce, lemon pepper, thyme, basil, parsley, and garlic powder in a bowl, and pour into a resealable plastic bag. Add the salmon fillets, coat with the marinade, squeeze out excess air, and seal the bag. Marinate in the refrigerator for at least 1 hour, turning occasionally.
2. Preheat an outdoor grill for medium heat, and lightly oil the grate. Remove the salmon from the marinade, and shake off excess. Discard the remaining marinade.
3. Grill the salmon on the preheated grill until browned and the fish flakes easily with a fork, about 5 minutes on each side.

MUSHROOM RISOTTO

Prep Time: 10 mins
Cook time: 35 mins
Servings: 4

NUTRITION

Calories: 439
Fat: 20g
Carbs: 49g
Protein: 17g

INGREDIENTS

- 1 tablespoon olive oil
- 3 small onions, finely chopped
- 1 clove garlic, crushed
- 1 teaspoon minced fresh parsley
- 1 teaspoon minced celery
- salt and pepper to taste
- 1 ½ cups sliced fresh mushrooms
- 1 cup whole milk
- ¼ cup heavy cream
- 1 cup rice
- 5 cups vegetable stock
- 1 teaspoon butter
- 1 cup grated Parmesan cheese

DIRECTION

1. Heat olive oil in a large skillet over medium-high heat. Saute the onion and garlic in the olive oil until onion is tender and garlic is lightly browned. Remove garlic, and stir in the parsley, celery, salt, and pepper. Cook until celery is tender, then add the mushrooms. Reduce heat to low, and continue cooking until the mushrooms are soft.
2. Pour the milk and cream into the skillet, and stir in the rice. Heat to a simmer. Stir the vegetable stock into the rice one cup at a time, until it is absorbed.
3. When the rice has finished cooking, stir in the butter and Parmesan cheese, and remove from heat. Serve hot.

SPICED LENTIL & BUTTERNUT SQUASH SOUP

Prep Time: 10 mins
Cook time: 40 mins
Servings: 4

NUTRITION

Kcal: 167
Fat: 5g
Saturates: 1g
Carbs: 23g
Sugars: 4g
Fibre: 3g
Protein: 6g
Salt: 0.5g

INGREDIENTS

- 2 tbsp olive oil
- 2 onions, finely chopped
- 2 garlic cloves, crushed
- ¼ tsp hot chilli powder
- 1 tbsp ras el hanout
- 1 butternut squash, peeled and cut into 2cm pieces
- 100g red lentils
- 1l hot vegetable stock
- 1 small bunch coriander, leaves chopped, plus extra to serve

dukkah (see tip) and natural yogurt, to serve

DIRECTION

1. Heat a large saucepan and dry-fry 2 tsp cumin seeds and a pinch of chilli flakes for 1 min, or until they start to jump around the pan and release their aromas.
2. Scoop out about half with a spoon and set aside. Add 2 tbsp olive oil, 600g coarsely grated carrots, 140g split red lentils, 1l hot vegetable stock and 125ml milk to the pan and bring to the boil.
3. Simmer for 15 mins until the lentils have swollen and softened.
4. Whizz the soup with a stick blender or in a food processor until smooth (or leave it chunky if you prefer).
5. Season to taste and finish with a dollop of plain yogurt and a sprinkling of the reserved toasted spices. Serve with warmed naan breads.

SPICED CARROT & LENTIL SOUP

Prep Time: 10 mins
Cook time: 15 mins
Servings: 4

NUTRITION

Kcal: 238
Fat: 7g
Saturates: 1g
Carbs: 34g
Sugars: 0g
Fibre: 5g
Protein: 11g
Salt: 0.25g

INGREDIENTS

- 2 tsp cumin seeds
- pinch chilli flakes
- 2 tbsp olive oil
- 600g carrots, washed and coarsely grated (no need to peel)
- 140g split red lentils
- 1l hot vegetable stock (from a cube is fine)
- 125ml milk (to make it dairy-free, see 'try' below)

plain yogurt and naan bread, to serve

DIRECTION

1. Heat a large saucepan and dry-fry 2 tsp cumin seeds and a pinch of chilli flakes for 1 min, or until they start to jump around the pan and release their aromas.
2. Scoop out about half with a spoon and set aside. Add 2 tbsp olive oil, 600g coarsely grated carrots, 140g split red lentils, 1l hot vegetable stock and 125ml milk to the pan and bring to the boil.
3. Simmer for 15 mins until the lentils have swollen and softened.
4. Whizz the soup with a stick blender or in a food processor until smooth (or leave it chunky if you prefer).
5. Season to taste and finish with a dollop of plain yogurt and a sprinkling of the reserved toasted spices. Serve with warmed naan breads.

TUNA FISH SALAD

Prep Time: 15 mins
Cook time: 15 mins
Servings: 4

INGREDIENTS

- 1 (5 ounce) can tuna, drained
- ½ cup mayonnaise
- ¼ cup chopped celery
- ¼ cup chopped onion
- 1 tablespoon chopped fresh parsley
- ½ teaspoon lemon juice
- ¼ teaspoon garlic powder
- ⅛ teaspoon salt
- ⅛ teaspoon ground black pepper
- 1 pinch paprika, or to taste

NUTRITION

Calories: 240
Fat: 22g
Carbs: 2g
Protein: 9g

DIRECTION

1. Gather all ingredients.
2. Combine tuna, mayonnaise, celery, onion, parsley, lemon juice, garlic powder, salt, and pepper in a large bowl; mix well. Season with paprika; refrigerate until chilled.

BUTTERNUT SQUASH CURRY

Prep Time: 10 mins
Cook time: 35 mins

Servings: 4

NUTRITION

Kcal: 238
Fat: 7g
Saturates: 1g
Carbs: 34g
Sugars: 0g
Fibre: 5g
Protein: 11g
Salt: 0.25g

INGREDIENTS

- 1 tablespoon olive oil, or as needed
- 1 medium butternut squash - peeled, seeded, and cubed
- 1 medium red onion, diced
- 2 tablespoons red curry paste
- 1 ¼ cups vegetable broth
- 4 medium tomatoes, chopped
- 1 (15 ounce) can chickpeas, drained
- salt and ground black pepper to taste
- 3 tablespoons Greek yogurt
- ½ tablespoon ground coriander

DIRECTION

1. Heat oil in a pot over medium heat. Add squash; cook and stir for 3 minutes. Add onion and curry paste; cook and stir for 4 minutes. Pour in vegetable broth, cover, and cook until squash is tender, about 20 minutes.
2. Stir tomatoes, chickpeas, salt, and pepper into the pot and cook until heated through, about 4 minutes. Stir in Greek yogurt and coriander.

SALMON WITH LEMON AND DIL

Prep Time: 10 mins

Cook time: 25 mins

Servings: 4

INGREDIENTS

- 1 pound salmon fillets
- ¼ cup butter, melted
- 5 tablespoons lemon juice
- 1 tablespoon dried dill weed
- ¼ teaspoon garlic powder
- sea salt to taste
- freshly ground black pepper to taste

NUTRITION

Calories: 186
Fat: 11g
Carbs: 5g
Protein: 16g

DIRECTION

1. Gather the ingredients. Preheat the oven to 350 degrees F (175 degrees C). Lightly grease a medium baking dish.
2. Place salmon in the baking dish.
3. Mix butter and lemon juice in a small bowl, and drizzle over salmon. Season with dill, garlic powder, sea salt, and pepper.
4. Bake in the preheated oven until salmon is easily flaked with a fork, about 25 minutes.
5. Serve and enjoy!

LENTIL SOUP

Prep Time: 10 mins
Cook time: 1hr 20 mins
Servings: 8

NUTRITION

Calories: 349
Fat: 10g
Carbs: 48g
Protein: 18g

INGREDIENTS

- ¼ cup olive oil
- 1 onion, chopped
- 2 carrots, diced
- 2 stalks celery, chopped
- 2 cloves garlic, minced
- 1 bay leaf
- 1 teaspoon dried oregano
- 1 teaspoon dried basil
- 2 cups dry lentils
- 8 cups water
- 1 (14.5 ounce) can crushed tomatoes
- ½ cup spinach, rinsed and thinly sliced
- 2 tablespoons vinegar
- salt to taste
- ground black pepper to taste

DIRECTION

1. Heat oil in a large soup pot over medium heat. Add onions, carrots, and celery; cook and stir until onion is tender, 3 to 5 minutes.
2. Stir in garlic, bay leaf, oregano, and basil; cook for 2 minutes.
3. Stir in lentils, and add water and tomatoes. Bring to a boil. Reduce heat and let simmer until lentils are tender, at least 1 hour.
4. When ready to serve, stir in spinach and cook until it wilts.
5. Stir in vinegar and season with salt and pepper; taste and adjust as needed.
6. Serve hot and enjoy!

RED LENTIL, CHICKPEA & CHILLI SOUP

Prep Time: 10 mins
Cook time: 25 mins
Servings: 4

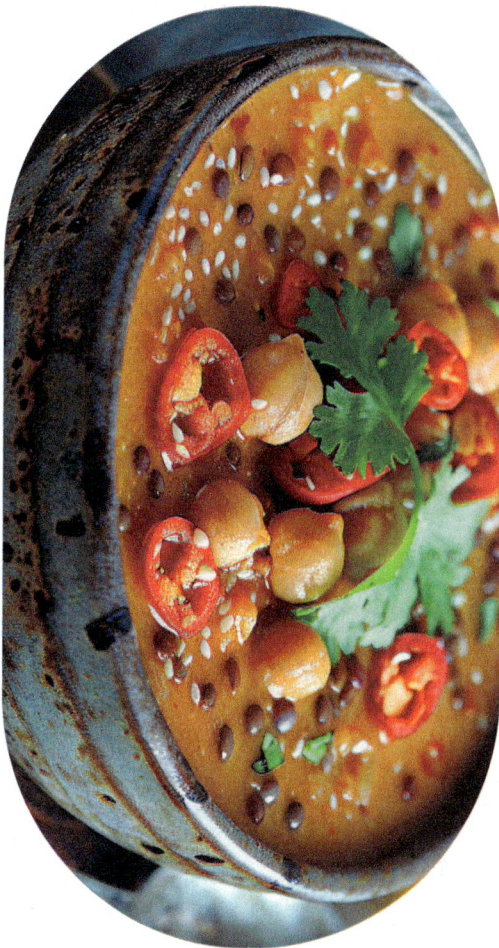

NUTRITION

Kcal: 222
Fat: 5g
Saturates: 0g
Carbs: 33g
Sugars: 6g
Fibre: 6g
Protein: 13g
Salt: 0.87g

INGREDIENTS

- 2 tsp cumin seeds
- large pinch chilli flakes
- 1 tbsp olive oil
- 1 red onion, chopped
- 140g red split lentils
- 850ml vegetable stock or water
- 400g can tomatoes, whole or chopped
- 200g can chickpeas or ½ a can, drained and rinsed (freeze leftovers)
- small bunch coriander, roughly chopped (save a few leaves, to serve)

4 tbsp 0% Greek yogurt, to serve

DIRECTION

1. Step 1: In a large casserole dish or saucepan, heat the oil over medium-high heat. Fry the onions with a pinch of salt for 7 minutes until they are softened and just caramelized. Add the garlic, chili, and ras el hanout, cooking for an additional minute.
2. Step 2: Add the squash and lentils. Pour in the stock and season to taste. Bring to a boil, then reduce the heat to a simmer and cook covered for 25 minutes, or until the squash is soft. Puree the soup with a stick blender until smooth, then season again to taste. If freezing, let it cool completely and transfer to large freezer-proof bags.
3. Step 3: Stir in the coriander leaves and ladle the soup into bowls. Serve topped with dukkah, yogurt, and extra coriander leaves.

TOMATO & PASTA SOUP

Prep Time: 5 mins
Cook time: 25 mins
Servings: 4

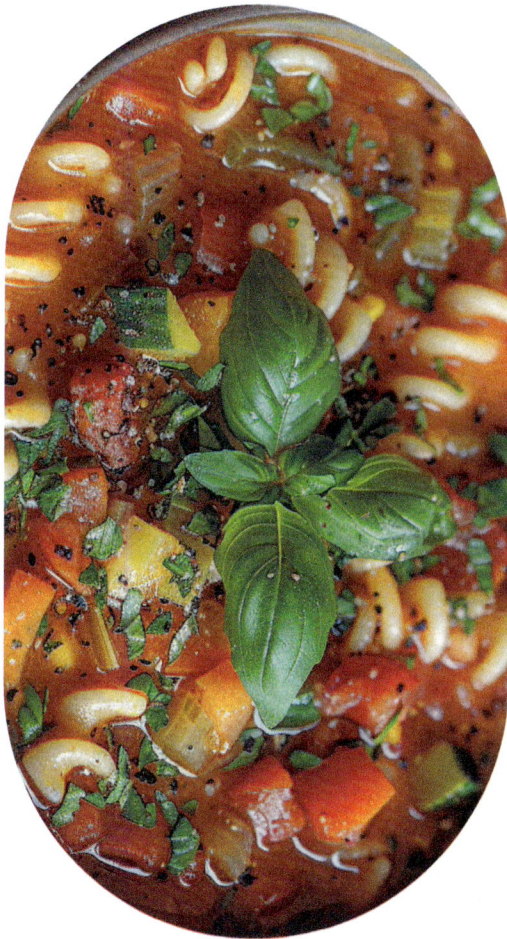

NUTRITION

Kcal: 349
Fat: 12g
Saturates: 2g
Carbs: 45g
Sugars: 9g
Fibre: 8g
Protein: 12g
Salt: 0.6g

INGREDIENTS

- 2 tbsp olive oil
- 1 onion, chopped
- 2 celery sticks, chopped
- 2 garlic cloves, crushed
- 1 tbsp tomato purée
- 400g can chopped tomatoes
- 400g can chickpeas
- 150g orzo or other small pasta shapes
- 700ml vegetable stock
- 2 tbsp basil pesto

crusty bread, to serve

DIRECTION

1. Heat 1 tbsp olive oil in a large saucepan. Add the onion and celery and fry for 10-15 mins, or until starting to soften, then add the garlic and cook for 1 min more. Stir in all the other ingredients, except for the pesto and remaining oil, and bring to the boil.
2. Reduce the heat and leave to simmer for 6-8 mins, or until the pasta is tender. Season to taste, then ladle into bowls.
3. Stir the remaining oil with the pesto, then drizzle over the soup. Serve with chunks of crusty bread.

PRAWN TIKKA MASALA

Prep Time: 5 mins
Cook time: 25 mins
Servings: 4

NUTRITION

Kcal: 432
Fat: 16g
Saturates: 3g
Carbs: 50g
Sugars: 12g
Fibre: 5g
Protein: 18g
Salt: 1.1g

INGREDIENTS

- 1 large onion, roughly chopped
- 1 thumb-sized piece ginger, peeled and grated
- 2 large garlic cloves
- 1 tbsp rapeseed oil
- 2-3 tbsp tikka curry paste
- 400g can chopped tomatoes
- 2 tbsp tomato purée
- ½ tbsp light brown soft sugar
- 3 cardamom pods, bashed
- 200g brown basmati rice
- 3 tbsp ground almonds
- 300g raw king prawns
- 1 tbsp double cream
- ½ bunch of coriander, roughly chopped

naan breads, warmed, to serve (optional)

DIRECTION

1. Blend onion, ginger, and garlic into a smooth paste in a food processor. Heat oil in a large casserole dish or pan over medium heat. Fry the onion paste for 8 minutes until lightly golden. Add curry paste and fry for another minute. Then, add tomatoes, tomato purée, sugar, and cardamom pods. Simmer covered for 10 minutes.

2. Cook the rice according to the package instructions.

3. Remove and discard the cardamom pods from the curry sauce, then blitz the sauce using a hand blender or in a clean food processor. Return the sauce to the pan, add almonds and prawns, and cook for 5 minutes. Season to taste, stir in the cream and coriander. Serve the curry with rice and naan breads, if desired.

LOW-FAT TURKEY BOLOGNESE

Prep Time: 5 mins
Cook time: 25 mins
Servings: 4

NUTRITION

Kcal: 267
Fat: 13g
Saturates: 3g
Carbs: 15g
Sugars: 12g
Fibre: 6g
Protein: 23g
Salt: 1.3g

INGREDIENTS

- 400g lean turkey mince (choose breast instead of thigh mince if you can, as it has less fat)
- 2 tsp vegetable oil
- 1 large onion, chopped
- 1 large carrot, chopped
- 3 celery sticks, chopped
- 250g pack brown mushroom, finely chopped
- pinch of sugar
- 1 tbsp tomato purée
- 2 x 400g cans chopped tomato with garlic & herbs
- 400ml chicken stock, made from 1 low-sodium stock cube

cooked wholemeal pasta and fresh basil leaves (optional), to serve

33

DIRECTION

1. Heat a large non-stick frying pan and dry-fry the turkey mince until browned. Tip onto a plate and set aside.
2. Add the oil and gently cook the onion, carrot and celery until softened, about 10 mins (add a splash of water if it starts to stick). Add the mushrooms and cook for a few mins, then add the sugar and tomato purée, and cook for 1 min more, stirring to stop it from sticking.
3. Add the tomatoes, turkey and stock with some seasoning. Simmer for at least 20 mins (or longer) until thickened. Serve with the pasta and fresh basil, if you have it.

APPLE ALMOND BUTTER DIP

🕐 Prep Time: 5 mins
🕐 Cook time: 25 mins
🍴 Servings: 4

INGREDIENTS

- 400g lean turkey mince (choose breast instead of thigh mince if you can, as it has less fat)
- 2 tsp vegetable oil
- 1 large onion, chopped
- 1 large carrot, chopped
- 3 celery sticks, chopped
- 250g pack brown mushroom, finely chopped
- pinch of sugar
- 1 tbsp tomato purée
- 2 x 400g cans chopped tomato with garlic & herbs
- 400ml chicken stock, made from 1 low-sodium stock cube

cooked wholemeal pasta and fresh basil leaves (optional), to serve

DIRECTION

1. Puree all ingredients in a small food processor until smooth. Transfer to a covered container and refrigerate until ready to serve. Serve with apple slices, grapes, banana slices, or strawberries.

SESAME & SPRING ONION STIR-FRIED UDON WITH CRISPY TOFU

 Prep Time: 5 mins
Cook time: 25 mins
Servings: 4

NUTRITION

Kcal: 267
Fat: 13g
Saturates: 3g
Carbs: 15g
Sugars: 12g
Fibre: 6g
Protein: 23g
Salt: 1.3g

INGREDIENTS

- 400g block firm tofu
- 1 tbsp cornflour
- ½ -1 tsp chilli flakes, to taste
- ¼-½ tsp Szechuan peppercorns, ground, to taste
- 1 tbsp vegetable oil
- bunch of spring onions, trimmed and cut into lengths
- 200g green beans, trimmed and cut into lengths
- 400g ready-to-use thick udon noodles
- ½ tbsp sesame oil
- 2 tsp sesame seeds, plus a pinch to serve
- 1 tbsp low-salt soy sauce, plus extra to serve

1 tbsp rice vinegar

DIRECTION

1. Drain the tofu and pat it dry with kitchen paper. Cut the tofu into cubes, wrap them in more kitchen paper, and place a heavy board on top to press and drain for 15 minutes.
2. in a bowl, mix cornflour, chili flakes, ground peppercorns, and a pinch of salt. Add the drained tofu and toss well to coat evenly.
3. Heat half of the vegetable oil in a large non-stick frying pan over high heat. Fry the tofu pieces for 5-6 minutes until golden on all sides, then remove and let them drain on kitchen paper.
4. In the same pan, add the remaining oil and stir-fry the spring onions and beans for 3-4 minutes until tender and lightly golden. Loosen noodles by pouring boiling water over them in a sieve. Drain the noodles well, then add them to the pan. Fry for a few more minutes until hot. Add sesame oil and sesame seeds, sizzle for a few seconds, then splash in soy sauce and rice vinegar. Add the fried tofu back into the pan, toss everything well, and serve in bowls. Garnish with a pinch of sesame seeds on top and offer more soy sauce on the side.

CELERY SOUP

NUTRITION

Calories: 208
Fat: 8g
Carbs: 32g
Protein: 5g

Prep Time: 30 mins

Cook time: 1hrs

Servings: 6

INGREDIENTS

- 3 tablespoons olive oil, divided, or to taste
- 1 large onion, chopped
- 2 carrots, peeled and chopped, or more to taste
- 1 leek, thinly sliced
- 4 cloves garlic, peeled and chopped
- 6 cups diced celery
- 1 quart chicken bone broth
- 1 ½ pounds baby yellow potatoes, peeled
- 1 small bunch fresh parsley
- 1 teaspoon dried thyme, or to taste
- ½ teaspoon salt-free seasoning blend (such as Penzeys Mural of Flavor), or to taste
- salt and ground black pepper to taste

DIRECTION

1. Heat 2 tablespoons olive oil in a frying pan over medium heat. Add onion, carrots, and leek; cook until soft, about 5 minutes. Add garlic; cook for 1 minute. Transfer to a soup pot.
2. Heat remaining olive oil in the same frying. Saute celery to release some of the moisture, about 10 minutes.
3. Transfer celery to the soup pot. Add chicken broth and potatoes. Cut parsley into the pot using kitchen scissors. Season soup with thyme, seasoning blend, salt, and pepper. Increase heat to medium-high and bring to a rolling simmer.
4. Reduce heat and simmer until carrots, celery, and potatoes are soft enough to easily puree, about 30 minutes. Avoid cooking vegetables until mushy. Remove from heat and cool for about 20 minutes.
5. Puree soup with an immersion blender. Simmer over low heat until heated through, 10 to 15 minutes. Serve immediately or let flavors meld overnight and serve the next day.

RUSTIC VEGETABLE SOUP

Prep Time: 15 mins
Cook time: 30 mins
Servings: 4

NUTRITION

Kcal: 162
Fat: 5g
Saturates: 1g
Carbs: 19g
Sugars: 9g
Fibre: 7g
Protein: 7g
Salt:0.4g

INGREDIENTS

- 1 tbsp rapeseed oil
- 1 large onion, chopped
- 2 carrots, chopped
- 2 celery sticks, chopped
- 50g dried red lentils
- 1½ l boiling vegetable bouillon (we used Marigold)
- 2 tbsp tomato purée
- 1 tbsp chopped fresh thyme
- 1 leek, finely sliced
- 175g bite-sized cauliflower florets
- 1 courgette, chopped
- 3 garlic cloves, finely chopped
- ½ large Savoy cabbage, stalks removed and leaves chopped

1 tbsp basil, chopped

DIRECTION

1. Heat the oil in a large pan with a lid. Add the onion, carrots and celery and fry for 10 mins, stirring from time to time until they are starting to colour a little around the edges. Stir in the lentils and cook for 1 min more.

2. Pour in the hot bouillon, add the tomato purée and thyme and stir well. Add the leek, cauliflower, courgette, and garlic, bring to the boil, then cover and leave to simmer for 15 mins.

3. Add the cabbage and basil and cook for 5 mins more until the veg is just tender. Season with pepper, ladle into bowls and serve. Will keep in the fridge for a couple of days. Freezes well. Thaw, then reheat in a pan until piping hot.

CREAMY GARLIC, LEMON & SPINACH SALMON

Prep Time: 5 mins

Cook time: 15 mins

Servings: 2

NUTRITION

Kcal: 162
Fat: 5g
Saturates: 1g
Carbs: 19g
Sugars: 9g
Fibre: 7g
Protein: 7g
Salt:0.4g

INGREDIENTS

- 2 sweet potatoes
- 1 tbsp olive oil or rapeseed oil
- 2 salmon fillets, skin removed
- 2 garlic cloves, thinly sliced
- 170g baby spinach
- 1 lemon, zested and ½ juiced, ½ thinly sliced
- 75g mascarpone
5 tbsp milk

DIRECTION

1. Preheat the oven to 200°C (180°C fan/gas mark 6). Pierce sweet potatoes a few times each and microwave on high for 5 minutes until soft, or alternatively bake for 35-40 minutes. Keep them warm until ready to serve.

2. In a frying pan, heat half the oil and lightly brown the salmon on both sides without fully cooking it through. Transfer the salmon to a plate, wipe out the pan, add the remaining oil, and briefly cook the garlic. Add spinach, lemon zest, and juice, and season. Mix in the mascarpone and 2 tablespoons of milk, cooking until the spinach wilts.

3. Transfer the spinach mixture into an ovenproof dish, top with lemon slices and salmon fillets, and bake for 5-8 minutes until the salmon is fully cooked.

4. Meanwhile, scoop out the flesh from the sweet potatoes, mash with the remaining milk and some seasoning. Serve this sweet potato mash alongside the baked salmon and creamy spinach.

PAN-FRIED SALMON

Prep Time: 1 mins

Cook time: 5 mins

Servings: 2

INGREDIENTS

- 2 tablespoons butter
- 2 tablespoons lemon juice
- 4 salmon fillets
- salt and freshly ground black pepper to taste

NUTRITION

kcal: 524
fat: 44
saturates: 15g
carbs: 0.3g
sugars: 0.3g
fibre: 0.3g
protein: 31g
salt: 0.17g

DIRECTION

1. Season the salmon fillets generously with salt and pepper.
2. In a non-stick frying pan, heat oil and butter over medium heat until melted and foaming, then increase the heat.
3. Once the butter bubbles, add the salmon, skin-side-down, and fry for 3 minutes until the skin is crisp.
4. Flip the fillets, reduce the heat, and cook for another 2 minutes, then drizzle with lemon juice.
5. Transfer the salmon to a plate and baste with the remaining buttery juices from the pan.

PRAWN & SALMON BURGERS WITH SPICY MAYO

🕐 Prep Time: 15 mins

🕐 Cook time: 10 mins

🍴 Servings: 4

NUTRITION

Kcal: 504
Fat: 36g
Saturates: 5g
Carbs: 4g
Sugars: 4g
Fibre: 3g
Protein: 39g
Salt: 0.7g

INGREDIENTS

- 180g pack peeled raw prawns, roughly chopped
- 4 skinless salmon fillets, chopped into small chunks
- 3 spring onions, roughly chopped
- 1 lemon, zested and juiced
- small pack coriander
- 60g mayonnaise or Greek yogurt
- 4 tsp chilli sauce (we used sriracha)
- 2 Little Gem lettuces, shredded
- 1 cucumber, peeled into ribbons
- 1 tbsp olive oil
4 seeded burger buns, toasted, to serve

DIRECTION

1. In a food processor, blitz half of the prawns, half of the salmon, spring onions, lemon zest, and half of the coriander until it forms a coarse paste. Transfer to a bowl, mix in the remaining prawns and salmon, season well, and shape into four burgers. Chill the burgers for 10 minutes.

2. In a small bowl, combine mayo and chilli sauce, season, and adjust the taste with some lemon juice. Separately, mix the lettuce with cucumber, dress with a little more lemon juice and 1 teaspoon of olive oil, then set aside.

3. Heat the remaining oil in a large frying pan and fry the burgers for 3-4 minutes on each side or until they develop a nice crust and the fish is cooked through. Serve the burgers with the salad on the side or in toasted burger buns, topped with a generous amount of the spicy mayo.

SALMON RISOTTO

Prep Time: 15 mins

Cook time: 1 hrs

Servings: 4

NUTRITION

Kcal: 806
Fat: 39g
Saturates: 14g
Carbs: 59g
Sugars: 6g
Fibre: 4g
Protein: 40g
Salt: 2g

INGREDIENTS

- 1 l chicken stock
- 4 salmon fillets
- 2 tbsp olive oil
- 50g butter
- 1 onion, very finely diced
- 1 garlic clove, crushed or finely grated
- 250g arborio rice
- 300ml white wine
- 100g frozen peas
- ½ lemon, juiced and zested
- 50g parmesan, grated, plus extra to serve

DIRECTION

1. Simmer chicken stock in a saucepan over medium heat. Add the salmon fillets and poach for 6 minutes or until just cooked. Remove the salmon, set aside to cool for 2-3 minutes, then remove the skin. Keep the stock warm.

2. Heat oil and half the butter in a large frying pan over medium-low heat. Once the butter melts, add the onion and cook for 10-12 minutes until softened but not browned. Add the garlic, cook for 1 minute, then stir in the rice and cook for 2 minutes until well coated in the oil.

3. Add wine, increase heat to medium, and cook until evaporated, about 4-5 minutes. Gradually add about a quarter of the reserved stock at a time to the rice, stirring frequently until each portion of stock is absorbed, about 4-5 minutes per addition. On the final addition of stock, add peas and flake in the cooked salmon. Season with black pepper and cook for 3-4 minutes until the rice is tender and everything is heated through. Add extra hot water if needed.

4. Remove the risotto from heat, stir in the remaining butter, lemon juice, and parmesan. Optionally, garnish with lemon zest and serve immediately.

AIR FRYER SALMON

Prep Time: 5 mins
Cook time: 8 mins
Servings: 4

NUTRITION

Kcal: 264
Fat: 17g
Saturates: 3g
Carbs: 0.1g
Sugars: 0g
Fibre: 0.1g
Protein: 27g
Salt: 1.36g

INGREDIENTS

- 1 tsp salt
- 1 tsp pepper
- 1 tsp mixed herbs
- 1 tsp garlic granules (optional)
- 4 salmon fillets (we used 4 x 130g fillets), skin on or removed
- ½ tbsp olive oil
- cooked seasonal greens and grains such as quinoa or brown rice, to serve (optional)

DIRECTION

1. Simmer chicken stock in a saucepan over medium heat. Add the salmon fillets and poach for 6 minutes or until just cooked. Remove the salmon, set aside to cool for 2-3 minutes, then remove the skin. Keep the stock warm.

2. Heat oil and half the butter in a large frying pan over medium-low heat. Once the butter melts, add the onion and cook for 10-12 minutes until softened but not browned. Add the garlic, cook for 1 minute, then stir in the rice and cook for 2 minutes until well coated in the oil.

3. Add wine, increase heat to medium, and cook until evaporated, about 4-5 minutes. Gradually add about a quarter of the reserved stock at a time to the rice, stirring frequently until each portion of stock is absorbed, about 4-5 minutes per addition. On the final addition of stock, add peas and flake in the cooked salmon. Season with black pepper and cook for 3-4 minutes until the rice is tender and everything is heated through. Add extra hot water if needed.

4. Remove the risotto from heat, stir in the remaining butter, lemon juice, and parmesan. Optionally, garnish with lemon zest and serve immediately.

PEA, FETA & SUMMER HERB FRITTATA

Prep Time: 15 mins
Cook time: 40 mins
Servings: 4

NUTRITION

Kcal: 337
Fat: 22g
Saturates: 9g
Carbs: 17g
Sugars: 4g
Fibre: 4g
Protein: 17g
Salt: 1.8g

INGREDIENTS

- 300g new potato (such as Jersey Royals), halved if large
- 4 eggs and 2 egg whites
- splash of milk
- 1 garlic clove, crushed
- 1 tbsp gluten-free wholegrain mustard
- handful mixed soft herbs, such as dill, mint and parsley, roughly chopped
- 3 tbsp cream cheese
- 1 tbsp olive oil
- 1 courgette, coarsely grated
- ½ tsp chilli flakes
- 140g petits pois (defrosted if frozen)
- 100g feta cheese, crumbled
- 50g sundried tomato, drained and roughly chopped
- 100g bag salad leaves, to serve

DIRECTION

1. Boil potatoes in salted water for 12-15 minutes until tender, then drain, cool, and thinly slice them. Whisk together eggs, egg whites, milk, garlic, mustard, herbs, and season well. Mix in cream cheese, leaving some lumps. Preheat the grill to medium-high.

2. In a 23cm non-stick frying pan, heat oil over medium heat. Fry the sliced potatoes for about 5 minutes until they start to turn golden. Add courgette and chili flakes, fry for a few more minutes, then stir in the petit pois.

3. Pour the egg mixture into the pan, scatter feta and tomatoes on top. Cook on a gentle heat for 10-12 minutes until almost set. Then, place the pan under the grill and cook for another 3-5 minutes until the frittata is puffed, golden, and cooked through. Serve in wedges with a crisp green salad.

SPICED CARROT & LENTIL SOUP

Prep Time: 10 mins

Cook time: 15 mins

Servings: 4

NUTRITION

Kcal: 238
Fat: 7g
Saturates: 1g
Carbs: 34g
Sugars: 0g
Fibre: 5g
Protein: 11g
Salt: 0.25g

INGREDIENTS

- 2 tsp cumin seeds
- pinch chilli flakes
- 2 tbsp olive oil
- 600g carrots, washed and coarsely grated (no need to peel)
- 140g split red lentils
- 1l hot vegetable stock (from a cube is fine)
- 125ml milk (to make it dairy-free, see 'try' below)
- plain yogurt and naan bread, to serve

DIRECTION

1. Heat a large saucepan and dry-fry 2 tsp cumin seeds and a pinch of chilli flakes for 1 min, or until they start to jump around the pan and release their aromas.
2. Scoop out about half with a spoon and set aside. Add 2 tbsp olive oil, 600g coarsely grated carrots, 140g split red lentils, 1l hot vegetable stock and 125ml milk to the pan and bring to the boil.
3. Simmer for 15 mins until the lentils have swollen and softened.
4. Whizz the soup with a stick blender or in a food processor until smooth (or leave it chunky if you prefer).
5. Season to taste and finish with a dollop of plain yogurt and a sprinkling of the reserved toasted spices. Serve with warmed naan breads.

VEGETABLE & BEAN CHILLI

Prep Time: 10 mins
Cook time: 15 mins
Servings: 4

NUTRITION

Kcal: 238
Fat: 7g
Saturates: 1g
Carbs: 34g
Sugars: 0g
Fibre: 5g
Protein: 11g
Salt: 0.25g

INGREDIENTS

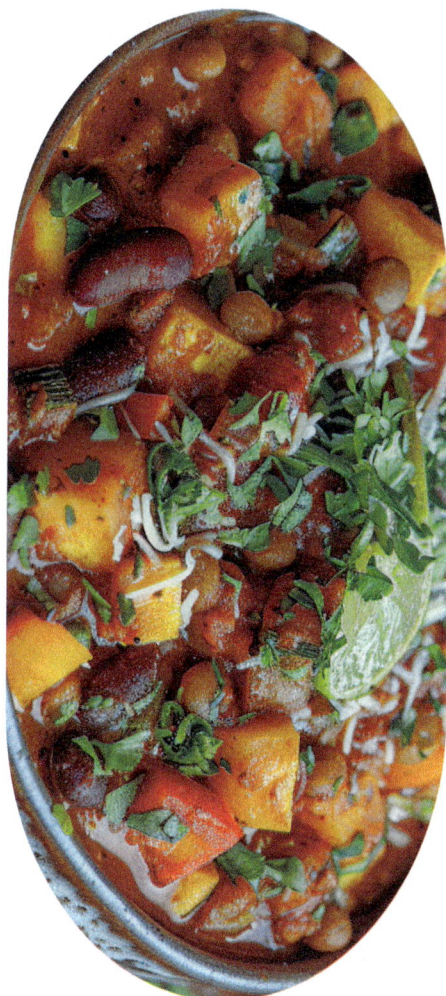

- 1tbsp olive oil
- 1 clove garlic, finely chopped
- ginger, finely chopped
- 1 large onion, chopped
- 2 courgettes, diced
- 1 red pepper, deseeded and chopped
- 1 yellow pepper, deseeded and chopped
- 1tbsp chilli powder
- 100g red lentils, washed and drained
- 1tbsp tomato purée
- 2x cans chopped tomatoes
- 195g can sweetcorn, drained
- 420g can butter beans, drained
- 400g can kidney beans in water, drained

DIRECTION

1. Heat the oil in a large pan. Cook the garlic, ginger, onion, courgettes and peppers for about 5 mins until starting to soften. Add the chilli powder and cook for 1 min more.
2. Stir in the lentils, tomato purée, tomatoes and 250ml water. Bring to the boil and cook for 15-20 mins.
3. Add the sweetcorn and beans, and cook for a further 10 mins.

WHOLE GRAIN BREAKFAST COOKIES

Prep Time: 25 mins
Cook time: 10 mins
Servings: 18

NUTRITION

Calories: 259
Fat: 16g
Carbs: 26g
Protein: 5g

INGREDIENTS

- 1 cup walnuts
- 1 ½ cups old-fashioned rolled oats (not instant)
- ⅓ cup whole wheat flour
- ½ cup ground flax meal
- 1 teaspoon baking soda
- ½ teaspoon salt
- 1 teaspoon ground cinnamon
- ½ cup almond butter
- ¼ cup canola oil
- ¼ cup blue agave nectar
- ⅓ cup brown sugar
- 1 egg
- 1 teaspoon vanilla extract
- ½ cup dried cherries
- 1 cup semi-sweet chocolate chips

DIRECTION

1. Preheat oven to 375 degrees F (190 degrees C). Line baking sheets with parchment paper.
2. Pulse the walnuts in a food processor several times to chop; continue processing until the walnuts are ground into flour; transfer to a bowl. Mix in the rolled oats, whole wheat flour, flax meal, baking soda, salt, and cinnamon until thoroughly combined.
3. Combine the almond butter, canola oil, agave nectar, brown sugar, egg, and vanilla extract in the food processor and process a few seconds to blend the ingredients well; transfer the almond butter mixture to a large bowl and fold in the dried cherries and chocolate chips. Mix the walnut-oatmeal mixture into the almond butter mixture (dough will be very thick).
4. Scoop up heaping teaspoons of dough, and form into balls; lay the dough balls onto the prepared baking sheets, about 2 inches apart.
5. Bake in the preheated oven until lightly browned, 8 to 10 minutes. Remove from oven and flatten the cookies with a spatula. Allow to cool for about 5 minutes on the baking sheets before removing to finish cooling on wire racks.

CHOCOLATE CHIA PUDDING

Prep Time: 25 mins

Cook time: 2 hrs

Servings: 1

INGREDIENTS

- 2 tablespoons cocoa powder
- 2 tablespoons brown sugar
- 1 teaspoon hazelnut flavor instant coffee powder (Optional)
- ¼ cup chia seeds
- 1 cup milk
- 2 teaspoons honey, or to taste

NUTRITION

Calories: 312
Fat: 7g
Carbs: 59g
Protein: 10g

DIRECTION

1. Mix cocoa powder, brown sugar, and instant coffee powder together in a bowl; stir until no lumps remain. Fold chia seeds into the mixture. Pour milk into the bowl and stir to incorporate; let the mixture sit a few minutes before stirring again. Repeat resting and stirring a few times over the course of 20 minutes.
2. Cover the bowl with plastic wrap and refrigerate 2 hours to overnight.
3. Drizzle honey over the pudding to serve.

CHIA PUDDING

Prep Time: 5 mins

Cook time: 8 hrs

Servings: 4

INGREDIENTS

- 2 cups milk
- ⅔ cup chia seeds
- 1 tablespoon white sugar
- ½ teaspoon vanilla extract
- 2 tablespoons unsweetened coconut flakes
- 2 tablespoons raisins

NUTRITION

Calories: 312
Fat: 7g
Carbs: 59g
Protein: 10g

DIRECTION

1. Combine milk, chia seeds, sugar, and vanilla in a bowl; let sit for about 10 minutes. Stir, then cover with plastic wrap and refrigerate, 8 hours to overnight.
2. Top the pudding with coconut and raisins to serve.

NUTS & SEEDS GRANOLA

Prep Time: 25 mins
Cook time: 10 mins
Servings: 18

NUTRITION

Calories: 259
Fat: 16g
Carbs: 26g
Protein: 5g

INGREDIENTS

- 150g rolled oats
- 150g mixed nuts (we used whole hazelnuts, flaked almonds and whole pecans)
- 50g mixed seeds (we used a mixed bag containing sunflower, pumpkin, hemp and golden linseed)
- 50g raisins
- 1 tsp ground cinnamon
- ¼ tsp sea salt
- 1 tsp almond extract (vanilla works well too, if you prefer)
- 50ml vegetable oil
- 100ml maple syrup
- milk or yogurt, and fruit (optional), to serve

DIRECTION

1. Preheat the oven to 180°C (160°C fan, gas mark 4). Line a large baking sheet with parchment paper. In a large mixing bowl, combine all the dry ingredients. In a jug, whisk together almond extract, vegetable oil, and maple syrup, then pour this mixture over the dry ingredients.

2. Thoroughly mix everything, ensuring all dry ingredients are well-coated and there are no dry spots. Spread the mixture evenly on the prepared baking sheet. Bake for about 25-30 minutes until golden, stirring every 8-10 minutes to ensure even drying and to prevent excessive clumping. Watch closely to avoid burning the nuts.

3. Remove the granola from the oven and allow it to cool completely on the tray. Break up any large clumps with a wooden spoon. Store in an airtight container for up to one month. Serve with milk or yogurt and fresh seasonal fruit, if desired.

CHIA & ALMOND OVERNIGHT OATS

Prep Time: 10 mins

Cook time: 5 mins

Servings: 4

NUTRITION

Kcalz; 370
Fat: 15g
Saturates: 3g
Carbs: 38g
Sugars: 8g
Fibre: 12g
Protein: 14g
Salt: 0.3g

INGREDIENTS

- 200g jumbo porridge oats
- 50g chia seeds
- 600ml unsweetened almond milk, plus 8 tbsp
- 2 tsp vanilla extract
- 125g punnet raspberries
- 100g almond yogurt
- 250g punnet blueberries
- 20g flaked almonds, toasted

DIRECTION

1. Combine oats and seeds in a bowl, pour over milk and vanilla extract. Let sit for 5-10 minutes to allow the oats to absorb some of the liquid.
2. Set aside 16 raspberries. Mash the remaining raspberries into the oat mixture. Divide and spoon the mixture into four tumblers or sundae dishes. Top with yogurt and both types of berries. Cover and refrigerate overnight or until ready to serve. To serve, pour 2 tablespoons of almond milk over each serving and sprinkle with almonds.

BANANA OAT PANCAKES

Prep Time: 5 mins
Cook time: 15 mins
Servings: 2

NUTRITION

Kcal: 350
Fat: 9.9g
Saturates: 2.5g
Carbs: 46g
Sugars: 9.8
Fibre: 5g
Protein: 15g
Salt: 1.4g

INGREDIENTS

- 125ml oat milk
- 2 eggs, separated
- 1 small banana
- 100g rolled oats
- 2 tsp baking powder
- few drops of vanilla extract
- oil, we used avocado oil spray
- low-fat yogurt and fruit to top

DIRECTION

1. Step 1: Blend oat milk, egg yolks, banana, oats, baking powder, and vanilla into a smooth mixture. Whisk egg whites to stiff peaks, mix a small amount into the batter to lighten it, then gently fold in the rest.

2. Step 2: Warm a non-stick pan over medium heat and lightly oil it. Pour about 2 tablespoons of batter per pancake and cook for 1-2 minutes until the base sets and bubbles form on top. Flip and cook for another minute. Repeat with the remaining batter, ensuring the pancakes are dry on top before flipping to prevent collapsing.

WHOLEMEAL FLATBREADS

Prep Time: 10 mins

Cook time: 10 mins

Servings: 8

NUTRITION

Kcal: 168
Fat: 2g
Saturates: 0g
Carbs: 27g
Sugars: 1g
Fibre: 5g
Protein: 6g
Salt: 0g

INGREDIENTS

- 350g wholemeal flour, plus extra for dusting
- 4 tsp cold-pressed rapeseed oil
- Our Most Popular Alternative
- Poached eggs with broccoli, tomatoes & wholemeal flatbread

DIRECTION

1. In a medium bowl, rub oil into the flour with your fingertips. Add 225ml of warm water, mix thoroughly, then knead the mixture until the dough is smooth and elastic.

2. On a lightly floured surface, divide the dough into eight balls. Roll out each ball into a thin circle about 22cm in diameter, using a floured rolling pin. Keep turning the dough and use more flour as needed to prevent sticking. Set the rolled-out flatbreads aside. You can freeze them at this point if you're making them ahead.

3. Heat a non-stick frying pan on high. Cook each flatbread for about 30 seconds on each side, pressing down with a spatula to help it puff up and cook through. The flatbreads should have light brown patches and be fairly dry but not crisp. Keep the cooked flatbreads warm by wrapping them in a clean tea towel until all are cooked and ready to serve.

FRESH ORANGE JUICE

Prep Time: 5 mins
Cook time: 5 mins
Servings: 3

INGREDIENTS

- 4 oranges

NUTRITION

Calories: 50
Fat: 0g
Carbs: 12g
Protein: 1g

DIRECTION

1. Gather all ingredients.
2. Lightly smack each orange on the counter. Cut each orange in half and squeeze juice into a glass.

SPINACH AND BANANA POWER SMOOTHIE

Prep Time: 5 mins
Cook time: 5 mins
Servings: 3

INGREDIENTS

- 1 cup plain soy milk
- ¾ cup packed fresh spinach leaves
- 1 large banana, sliced

NUTRITION

Calories: 257
Fat: 5g
Carbs: 47g
Protein: 10g

DIRECTION

1. Gather all ingredients.
2. Blend soy milk and spinach together in a blender until smooth.
3. Add banana and pulse until thoroughly blended.

HELP-YOURSELF
TUNA RICE SALAD

Prep Time: 10 mins
Cook time: 10 mins
Servings: 8

NUTRITION

Kcal: 328
Fat: 10g
Saturates: 2g
Carbs: 49g
Sugars: 5g
Fibre: 2g
Protein: 14g
Salt: 0.22

INGREDIENTS

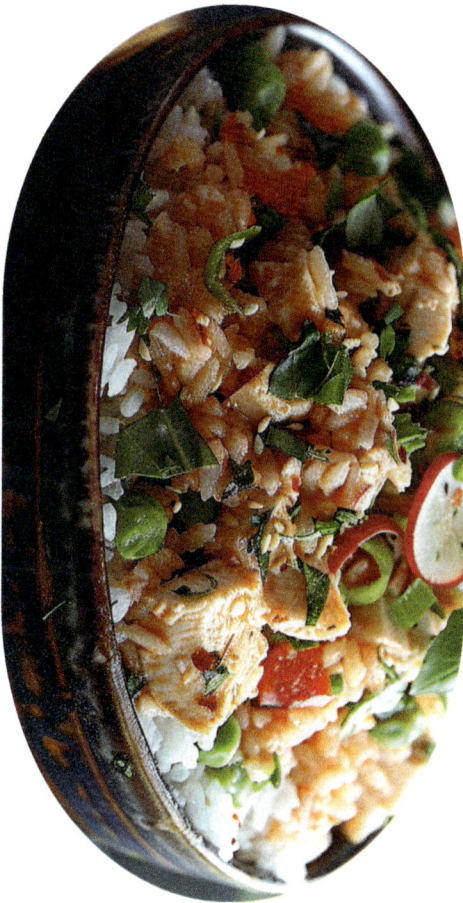

- approx 900g/2lb cold cooked rice (about 400g/14oz uncooked rice)
- 400g tuna in springwater
- 200g frozen petits pois, defrosted
- 2 red peppers, peeled with a potato peeler, deseeded and diced
- 3 tomatoes, chopped into small chunks
- 5 spring onions, finely sliced
- bunch flat-leaf parsley, chopped
- large handful stoned green olives, roughly chopped (optional)
- 4 tbsp mayonnaise
- juice 1 lemon
- 2 tbsp extra-virgin olive oil

DIRECTION

1. The cooked rice will have probably clumped together, so break it up in a large mixing bowl. Flake in the tuna, then mix in the peas, peppers, tomatoes, spring onions, parsley and olives, if you're using them.
2. Stir through the mayonnaise, lemon juice and olive oil and season to taste. Cover the bowl with cling film or place in a large plastic container and let your household serve themselves whenever they are hungry.

ORANGE-PEAR GREEN SMOOTHIE WITH BOK CHOY

Prep Time: 10 mins
Cook time: 10 mins
Servings: 2

INGREDIENTS

- 1 pear, cored
- 1 cup green grapes
- ⅓ cup water
- ½ cup chopped fresh pineapple
- ½ banana, frozen
- ½ cup chopped bok choy
- ½ cup chopped kale
- 1 orange, peeled
- ice
- 2 tablespoons chopped fresh mint

NUTRITION

Calories: 170
Fat: 1g
Carbs: 43g
Protein: 2g

DIRECTION

1. Combine pear, grapes, water, pineapple, banana, bok choy, kale, orange, ice, and mint in a large blender. Blend, starting on low speed and increasing to high, until smooth. Turn blender to liquefy setting for a smoother texture.

KALE, BANANA, AND PEANUT BUTTER SMOOTHIE

INGREDIENTS

- 2 bananas, cut into small chunks
- 1 ½ cups unsweetened vanilla-flavored almond milk
- ½ bunch kale - stems removed and discarded, leaves torn into bite-size pieces
- 4 cubes ice, or more if desired
  1 tablespoon peanut butter

NUTRITION

Calories: 563
Fat: 15g
Carbs: 105g
Protein: 16g

DIRECTION

1. Blend bananas, almond milk, kale, ice, and peanut butter in a blender until smooth.

BERRIES AND SPINACH SMOOTHIE

Prep Time: 10 mins
Cook time: 10 mins
Servings: 4

INGREDIENTS

- 2 cups frozen berries
- 1 cup plain yogurt
- ½ cup orange juice
- ¼ cup fresh spinach, or to taste
- 5 strawberries

NUTRITION

Calories: 88
Fat: 1g
Carbs: 17g
Protein: 4g

DIRECTION

1. Blend berries, yogurt, orange juice, spinach, and strawberries together in a blender until smooth.

WATERMELON REFRESHING GREEN SMOOTHIE

Prep Time: 10 mins
Cook time: 10 mins
Servings: 1

INGREDIENTS

- 2 cups diced watermelon
- ½ cup fresh spinach
- ¼ cup broccoli florets
- ¼ cucumber, sliced
- ½ apple - peeled, cored, and diced, or more to taste
- 1 stalk celery, coarsely chopped

NUTRITION

Calories: 64
Fat: 0g
Carbs: 15g
Protein: 2g

DIRECTION

1. Place watermelon in a blender; mix until liquefied. Add spinach, broccoli, cucumber, apple, and celery; blend until smooth.

SOYBEAN MILK

Prep Time: 1hrs
Cook time: 30 mins
Servings: 6

INGREDIENTS

- 1 ¾ cups dried soybeans
- 2 quarts water
- 1 pandan leaf
- 1 slice fresh ginger root
- 1 teaspoon vanilla extract
- ½ cup white sugar

NUTRITION

Calories: 309
Fat: 11g
Carbs: 33g
Protein: 20g

DIRECTION

1. Soak beans overnight in water. Drain, rinse, and discard water. Combine soaked beans with 2 quarts fresh water. In a food processor or blender, process beans with water until smooth.
2. Strain into a pot through a double layer of cheesecloth, or a fine sieve. Add pandan leaf or ginger, and sugar to taste. Boil soy milk for 15 minutes. Stir frequently to prevent skin from forming. Remove pandan leaf or ginger, then flavor with vanilla. Stir in sugar to taste. Cool to room temperature, then refrigerate.

GROOVY GREEN SMOOTHIE

INGREDIENTS

- 1 banana, cut in chunks
- 1 cup grapes
- 1 (6 ounce) tub vanilla yogurt
- ½ apple, cored and chopped
- 1 ½ cups fresh spinach leaves

NUTRITION

Calories: 205
Fat: 2g
Carbs: 45g
Protein: 6g

DIRECTION

1. Place the banana, grapes, yogurt, apple and spinach into a blender. Cover, and blend until smooth, stopping frequently to push down anything stuck to the sides. Pour into glasses and serve.

NICOISE-STYLE TUNA SALAD WITH WHITE BEANS & OLIVES

Prep Time: 10 mins

Cook time: 10 mins

Servings: 4

INGREDIENTS

- ¾ pound green beans, trimmed and snapped in half
- 1 (12 ounce) can solid white albacore tuna, drained
- 1 (16 ounce) can Great Northern beans, drained and rinsed
- 1 (2.25 ounce) can sliced black olives, drained
- ¼ medium red onion, thinly sliced
- 1 teaspoon dried oregano
- 6 tablespoons extra-virgin olive oil
- 3 tablespoons lemon juice
- ½ teaspoon finely grated lemon zest
- Salt and ground black pepper, to taste
- 4 large hard-cooked eggs, peeled and quartered

NUTRITION

Calories: 548
Fat: 30g
Carbs: 33g
Protein: 36g

DIRECTION

1. Place green beans, 1/3 cup water and a large pinch of salt in a medium skillet. Cover, turn heat on high, and bring water to boil. Once beans start to steam, set timer and cook until tender-crisp, about 5 minutes. (Because the beans cook in such a small amount of water, make sure not to let the skillet run dry.) Immediately dump them onto a lipped cookie sheet lined with paper towels to cool.

2. Mix tuna, white beans, olives and onion in a medium bowl. Whisk together oregano, oil, lemon juice and zest in a medium bowl, then pour over the salad and gently stir to combine.

3. Adjust seasonings to taste. Arrange a portion of green beans, tuna-bean salad and eggs on each of 4 plates.

SUPERHEALTHY
SALMON BURGERS

Prep Time: 20 mins

Cook time: 10 mins

Servings: 4

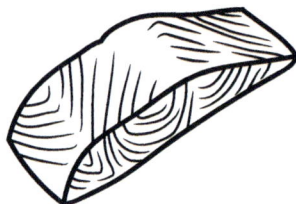

INGREDIENTS

- 4 boneless, skinless salmon fillets, about 550g/1lb 4oz in total, cut into chunks
- 2 tbsp Thai red curry paste
- thumb-size piece fresh root ginger, grated
- 1 tsp soy sauce
- 1 bunch coriander, half chopped, half leaves picked
- 1 tsp vegetable oil
- lemon wedges, to serve

For the salad
- 2 carrots
- half large or 1 small cucumber
- 2 tbsp white wine vinegar
- 1 tsp golden caster sugar

NUTRITION

Kcal: 292
Fat: 17g
Saturates: 4g
Carbs: 7g
Sugars: 6g
Fibre: 0g
Protein: 29g
Salt: 0.83g

DIRECTION

1. Tip the salmon into a food processor with the paste, ginger, soy and chopped coriander. Pulse until roughly minced. Tip out the mix and shape into 4 burgers. Heat the oil in a non-stick frying pan, then fry the burgers for 4-5 mins on each side, turning until crisp and cooked through.

2. Meanwhile, use a swivel peeler to peel strips of carrot and cucumber into a bowl. Toss with the vinegar and sugar until the sugar has dissolved, then toss through the coriander leaves. Divide the salad between 4 plates. Serve with the burgers and rice.

ROASTED CAULIFLOWER WITH TOMATO & CASHEW SAUCE

Prep Time: 20 mins

Cook time: 10 mins

Servings: 4

INGREDIENTS

- 1 cauliflower, cut into florets
- 2 tsp nigella seeds
- 2 tbsp vegetable oil
- 3 tsp garam masala
- 2 garlic cloves, crushed
- 2cm piece ginger, grated
- 500g passata
- 2 tbsp cashew nut butter
- 50ml double cream or single cream or plain yogurt
- To serve
- brown rice or naan bread
- ½ bunch coriander, chopped

NUTRITION

Kcal: 240
Fat: 17g
Saturates: 5g
Carbs: 13g
Sugars: 8g
Fibre: 3g
Protein: 7g
Salt: 0.1g

DIRECTION

1. Heat oven to 200C/180C fan/gas 6. Toss the cauliflower florets with the nigella seeds, 1 tbsp of the oil and 2 tsp of the garam masala. Spread out onto a roasting tray and cook for 35-40 mins until starting to soften and char, tossing halfway through.
2. Meanwhile, heat the rest of the oil in a small pan. Add the garlic, ginger, passata and the remaining garam masala and leave to simmer, uncovered, for 10-15 mins. Stir in the cashew nut butter (or peanut butter) and cream, then season to taste.
3. Serve the sauce over the brown rice or naan bread, top with the roasted cauliflower and garnish with the coriander.

GINGERY BROCCOLI-FRY WITH CASHEWS

Prep Time: 15 mins

Cook time: 10 mins

Servings: 2

NUTRITION

Kcal: 388
Fat: 21g
Saturates: 4g
Carbs: 22g
Sugars: 15g
Fibre: 13g
Protein: 20g
Salt: 1g

INGREDIENTS

- 320g head of broccoli, stalks and florets separated
- 40g cashews, roughly chopped
- 1 tbsp sesame oil
- 15g ginger, finely sliced
- 1 small red onion, finely chopped
- 1 red pepper, deseeded and cut into thin strips
- 1 large carrot (160g), cut into thin strips
- 2 garlic cloves, thinly sliced
- 1 red chilli, deseeded and finely chopped, plus extra sliced, to serve
- 1 tbsp tamari
- 1 lime, juiced and zested
- 7g chopped coriander, plus extra to serve
- 2 eggs, beaten

DIRECTION

1. Blitz the broccoli stalks in a food processor until finely chopped. Add the florets and pulse again to achieve a rice-like texture.
2. Lightly toast the cashews in a wok or frying pan, then tip onto a plate and set aside. Heat the oil in a pan over a high heat and add the ginger, onion, pepper, carrot, garlic and chilli. Stir-fry for 2-3 mins until starting to brown, then put a lid on and cook for another 2 mins.
3. Add the broccoli and 3 tbsp water and stir-fry for 3 mins until all the veg is tender. Pour in the tamari, lime juice and zest and coriander, stir well, then pour in the eggs and stir-fry very briefly to just set. Serve with the cashews, extra coriander and extra sliced chilli scattered over, if you like.

RED LENTIL & SQUASH DHAL

Prep Time: 15 mins

Cook time: 40 mins

Servings: 4

INGREDIENTS

- 1 tbsp sunflower oil
- 1 onion, finely chopped
- 1 garlic clove, finely chopped
- 1 tsp ground coriander
- 1 tsp ground cumin
- 1 tsp ground turmeric
- ½ tsp cayenne pepper
- 400g butternut squash, peeled and cut into 2cm (prepared weight)
- 400g can chopped tomato
- 1.2l chicken stock
- 1 heaped tbsp mango chutney
- 300g red lentil
- small pack coriander, roughly chopped
- naan bread, to serve

NUTRITION

Kcal: 495
Fat: 12g
Saturates: 2g
Carbs: 58g
Sugars: 14g
Fibre: 9g
Protein: 42g
Salt: 0.6g

DIRECTION

1. Put the oil and the onion in a saucepan, and cook for 5 mins. Stir in the garlic and cook for a further 1 min, then stir in the spices and butternut squash. Combine everything together.
2. Tip in the chopped tomatoes, stock and chutney, and season well. Bring to the boil, then gently simmer for about 10 mins. Add the lentils and simmer for another 20 mins until the lentils and squash are tender. Stir in the coriander and serve with warmed naan bread.

ROASTED RADISHES

Prep Time: 15 mins
Cook time: 15 mins
Servings: 4

INGREDIENTS

- 2 bunches radishes, trimmed
- 2 tablespoons extra-virgin olive oil
- 1 teaspoon ground thyme
- salt to taste
- ½ lemon, juiced

NUTRITION

Calories: 64
Fat: 0g
Carbs: 15g
Protein: 2g

DIRECTION

1. Preheat oven to 450 degrees F (230 degrees C). Line a baking sheet with aluminum foil.
2. Cut radishes into halves; cut any large radishes into quarters. Stir olive oil and thyme together in a bowl and toss radishes in mixture to coat. Spread radishes onto prepared baking sheet; sprinkle with salt.
3. Roast in the preheated oven until tender but firm in the centers, tossing every 5 minutes, 15 to 20 minutes. Drizzle with lemon juice.

BROCCOLI SALAD

Prep Time: 10 mins
Cook time: 15 mins
Servings: 8

NUTRITION

Calories: 374
Fat: 27g
Carbs: 29g
Protein: 7g

INGREDIENTS

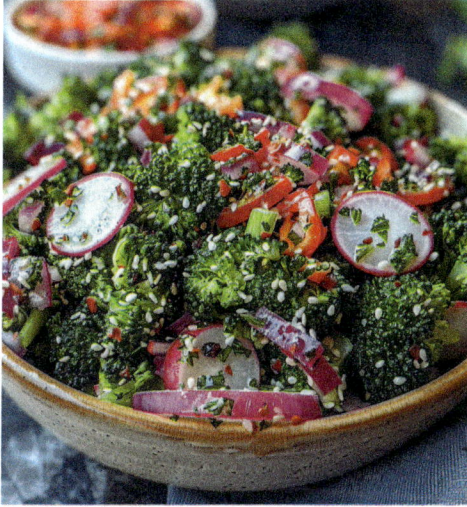

- ½ pound bacon
- 2 heads fresh broccoli, cut into bite-sized pieces
- 1 small red onion, sliced into bite-sized pieces
- ¾ cup raisins
- ¾ cup sliced almonds
- 1 cup mayonnaise
- ½ cup white sugar
- 2 tablespoons white wine vinegar

DIRECTION

1. Gather all ingredients.
2. Place bacon in a deep skillet and cook over medium-high heat until evenly brown, 7 to 10 minutes; drain, cool, and crumble.
3. Combine bacon, broccoli, onion, raisins, and almonds together in a bowl; mix well.
4. To prepare the dressing: Mix mayonnaise, sugar, and vinegar together until smooth.
5. Stir into the salad.
6. Let chill before serving, if desired.

91

GINGERY BROCCOLI-FRY WITH CASHEWS

Prep Time: 10 mins

Cook time: 5 mins

Servings: 4

INGREDIENTS

- 1 tbsp sesame seeds, lightly toasted
- 1 tsp poppy seeds
- 1 head of broccoli, cut into florets
- 100g frozen peas
- For the dressing
- 1 tbsp soy sauce
- 1 tsp clear honey
- ¼ tsp sesame oil

NUTRITION

Kcal: 68
Fat: 3g
Saturates: 0g
Carbs: 5g
Sugars: 3g
Fibre: 3g
Protein: 5g
Salt: 0.7g

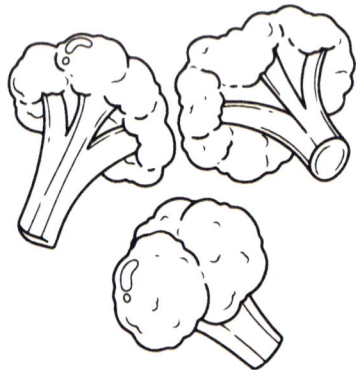

DIRECTION

1. To make the dressing, mix the soy, honey and sesame oil together. Mix the seeds together. Boil the broccoli and peas for 2 mins, then drain.

2. Tip the broccoli and peas back in the pan, pour half the dressing and half the seeds over, and shake for a few secs. Serve sprinkled with the rest of the dressing and seeds.

Printed in Great Britain
by Amazon

58601152R00056